Unlacing the Heart

Unlacing the Heart

Connecting with what really matters

HENRY B. FREEMAN, Ph.D.

FOREWORD BY JOHN STEWART

"Packed with heart-wisdom, Henry Freeman invites us into precious, heart-stretching, truthful, abrasive, and deep life encounters with men and women from the highest echelons of society to the homeless and alienated of the streets. The feelings are poignant, deep, and true. I have read this book twice and love every page. Truly wonderful writing!"

—Sue Mosteller, CSJ, The Henri Nouwen Society

JOHN'S PRESS, NORTH CAROLINA

www.unlacingtheheart.com

Library of Congress Number
ISBN-13 978-0-9962462-1-7

Copyright ©2015 by H. Freeman Associates, LLC

Published by John's Press, Brevard, N.C.

For more information:
    www.unlacingtheheart.com
       (speaking engagements and publications)
    www.hfreemanassociates.com
       (fundraising, training, and organization development services)

Design by Ellen C. Dawson and Blaise Freeman

Sources for material cited in text:

Chapter 1 epigraph: Parker J. Palmer, *The Active Life* (NY: Harper & Row, 1990), p. 98.

Chapter 2 epigraph: William Sloane Coffin, referenced by Ed O'Donnell based on his memory of a sermon presented by Reverend Coffin at Riverside Church, NYC, in the late 1970s.

Chapter 6 epigraph: Henri J. M. Nouwen, *A Spirituality of Fundraising* (Nashville: Upper Room Books, 2010), p. 49.

Chapter 6, epigraph beneath subhead: Henri J. M. Nouwen, *A Spirituality of Fundraising* (Nashville: Upper Room Books, 2010), p. 36.

Chapter 6, quotation at end of chapter: Henri J. M. Nouwen, *Reaching Out* (Doubleday, 1975), p. 16.

Chapter 13 epigraph: William B. Oglesby, cited by Richard L. Morgan, *Autumn Wisdom: A Book of Readings* (Nashville: Upper Room Books, 1995), p. 96.

Chapter 13, poem "Small White Cannibal": Grace Beacham Freeman, *No Costumes or Masks* (Brevard, N.C.: John's Press, 1986), p. 26.

What others are saying about
Unlacing the Heart: Connecting with what really matters

"This is a powerful and deeply moving work. Through the sharing of personal life stories, noted fundraiser Henry Freeman takes us on a journey that leads us to understand that everyone is special, and that wisdom can come from anywhere. This book will be an inspiration for anyone who has a servant's heart, and a desire to make a difference in the world."

—**Larry C. Spears**, author-editor,
Insights on Leadership,
The Spirit of Servant-Leadership

"In this book Freeman gifts us with a window into what it means to be human and truly present in our interactions with each other. Via poignant autobiographical vignettes, he reminds us that the fine art of fundraising begins with listening and the creation of a safe space where trust is nurtured, permitting donors to unlace their hearts and share their own sacred stories. This book will be a transformational read for fundraisers, development officers and philanthropists."

—**William G. Enright**, Ph.D.
Senior Fellow, Lake Institute on Faith & Giving
IUPUI Lilly Family School of Philanthropy

www.unlacingtheheart.com

"As someone who thought he knew Henry Freeman well, and in fact was the Earlham College president who turned down the resignation with which this wonderful book begins, I found surprising insights on almost every page—insights about him, about the human condition, about caring, about my own empty spaces, and about responding to that of God in every person."

—**Richard J. Wood**, Ph.D.
   President, Earlham College (1985–1996)
   Dean, Yale Divinity School (1996–2000)

"These extraordinary stories, offered by an otherwise ordinary man, demonstrate the remarkable and transforming power of grace. Rich or poor, learned or uneducated, strong or weak— Henry Freeman sees the beauty and even a spark of God alive in the people he meets, especially those who are otherwise invisible—the overlooked, ignored, or taken for granted. This rare quality reminds me of Jesus, the Master at seeing such invisible people and one who consistently came alongside each with compassion and grace. Though admittedly shy about voicing his faith, he works to incarnate this same spirit, and through these stories, gently nudges the rest of us to do the same."

—**Colin Saxton**, General Secretary,
   Friends United Meeting

"The reality of our common humanity, and the truth that we need each other, that the author so powerfully presents stands in stark contrast to our world so frequently filled with apathy and superficial conversation. As a fundraiser and former campus pastor, I resonate deeply with Henry Freeman's wise counsel that being authentically present in our relationships—by risking vulnerability—is the greatest gift we can offer another person. In moments of true blessing these genuine interactions also engender the greatest gifts we can receive."

—Timothy McElwee,
Vice President for Advancement
Manchester University

This book is dedicated to my friend Alfredo, who gave me the gift of knowing that one of our deepest longings is to find a safe place to take down our walls, be present with another human being and share our life story.

Alfredo. ?–1994

Contents

Acknowledgments

My ability to hear and share the stories in this book is grounded in the support I have always received from my parents, three siblings, and grandfather Beacham. Now in my adult years, I am also lifted up and embraced by my wife Sandy, our four children, their spouses, Uncle Tim, and a joyful package of grandchildren who are an important part of my life. Without my family, this book would not be possible.

As a consultant, my life has been enriched by many clients, most notably three clients with whom I have worked for fifteen or more years: Pendle Hill, Friends General Conference, and White's. I am also deeply appreciative for the advice and insights received from the following people who reviewed early drafts: Jennifer Karsten, Michael Gagné, Sarah Deschamps, Anne Harper, Amy Greulich, Christina Repoley, Dean Leeper, Theron Shaw, Larry Spears, Bill Enright, Tim McElwee, Richard Wood, Katharine Myers, Colin Saxton, Jim Thorne, Roland Kreager, Mike Johnson, Michael O'Laughlin, Jerry Toomer, Margaret Sorrel and the ten members of the Tuesday Discussion Group in Brevard, North Carolina. I also owe thanks to Ellen Dawson and Blaise Freeman for their design skills and John Stewart for his willingness to write the Foreword and narrate the audio edition of this work.

As the manuscript neared completion I became increasingly aware of the impact of my very first client on this work. That client was Sojourners—a Washington faith-based nonprofit that welcomed me both as a consultant with skills to share and as a person whose life had been transformed by the El Salvador stories included in these pages. The early years of our seventeen year partnership provided rich and fertile ground for exploring the important questions about wealth, human vulnerability, and the value of all people that are at the heart of this book. I am deeply grateful to Jim Wallis and the staff at Sojourners (both past and present) for the silent yet important role Sojourners has played in the sharing of these stories.

Lastly, I want to express my appreciation to Sue Mosteller, the literary executrix of Henri Nouwen's estate, and my brother David Freeman for taking the time (at their own expense!) to spend a weekend with me at Pendle Hill getting me back on track and convincing me that this book needed to be written.

Foreword

John Stewart, Ph.D.

Jewish scholars call the books of Job, Proverbs, and
Ecclesiastes "Wisdom Literature," because they contain
important reflections on the human condition and clar-
ify how people ought to live in God's world.

This book is wisdom literature.

The fact that it is written by a man whose profession is fundraising is a delicious and potent irony
because, as Henry Freeman writes, "The reality is that
most people do not want to connect with me or any
other fundraiser at more than a rather superficial level."
One doesn't expect to find sparkling, life-giving water
on what looks like an arid island. This irony enriches
the book's insights.

Unlacing the Heart is a book of stories—of Alfredo, a
crippled, diseased, homeless Salvadoran who profoundly
befriended Henry; of the distinguished theologian Henri
J. M. Nouwen, who taught the human importance of deep
listening by living it; of Herb Cahoon, Yale's director of
volunteer services, who modeled respectful vulnerability;

of Sister Margaret, who acknowledged the humanity of even the dangerous and scowling Salvadoran soldiers; of a soup kitchen regular also named Henry who showed what it means to be affirmed unconditionally by another person; of a prospective donor also named Margaret, who helped Henry Freeman learn the "need to always make space for what is in the heart of the people who welcome me into their lives."

Like all gifted storytellers, Freeman recounts these stories in passionate and evocative prose. Listen to one chapter's conclusion:

> So there we sat—a 43-year-old North American man with tears in his eyes and a small Salvadoran boy with tears buried deep in his heart. Two of God's wounded children, a man and a little boy, tenderly holding hands and comforting each other.

The reason that *Unlacing the Heart* is made up mainly of stories is that narrative is one of the best ways—and sometimes the only way—to say what Henry Freeman has to say to us: That what *really matters* in human lives are moments of direct, personal contact. That nothing is more important to the quality of our lives than our relationships, and nothing is more important to our relationships than our vulnerable presence to another human being. That being part of another's life adds *wholeness* to our own. That even an academic world can be experienced "not as volumes of information surrounded by complicated words but through simple questions about small moments in an ordinary person's life." That "a dream cannot be one person's alone," and "the owner of the dream must see him or herself as a vessel for uncovering how and where the dream also resides in other people." That relationships build when conversation partners are "able to explore the sacred space that connect[s] us as human beings."

Henry honored me with the invitation to write this Foreword, when we discovered that we are laboring in the same vineyard. From very different academic, professional, and personal backgrounds, he and I have discovered very similar truths about the human condition and how people ought to live in God's world. And as senior professionals, each of us is called to invite, not just academics, professionals, or students, but everyone in earshot to consider these truths.

In many ways, Henry and I are spitting into the wind, pushing the river. Local and national politics are hopelessly polarized. Race and class conflicts wound U.S. culture, and religious wars kill hundreds of thousands in the Middle East, Africa, and Southeast Asia. Stable families are a rarity. And much of the incred-

ible, world-wide power of technology and the inter-
net serves to depersonalize the ways humans treat each
other. Where is the place for the messages that are so
important to Henry and to me?

The fact that you are reading these words gives us
hope. Enjoy these pages, and take to heart what Henry
says. If you believe what's here is important, search for
ways to integrate it into your daily life. As often as you
can—at work, at home, while traveling, in meetings,
on social media—attend to people from the outside
in. Listen from your heart. Practice mindful presence.
Whenever it's possible—and sometimes when it seems
not to be—invite your conversation partner to make your
communicating as personal as possible.

The oppressively toxic, depersonalized culture we
inhabit was created and is sustained by people just like
us. And, as Henry Freeman shows, it can be dismantled,
one genuine human connection at a time.

John Stewart is Emeritus Professor of Communication at the University of Dubuque, and for
thirty-two years played a similar role at the University
of Washington. A specialist in interpersonal
communication, John has been an executive trainer
for Fortune 500 companies and has extensive
experience working with both non-profit and
for-profit organizations in the areas of team building,

group facilitation, dialogue, and communication ethics. An award-winning author, teacher and communication consultant, his best known work *Bridges Not Walls* has sold over half a million copies.

Introduction

"The marvelous thing about learning
from a story is that the story never ends, so
our learning from it need not end either."

—Parker J. Palmer

This book is written as a series of small windows into the lives of people at very vulnerable points on their life journeys. While each story reflects a special moment in time and space, an invisible thread weaves and binds each of the stories together.

That thread is not a carefully thought-out plot or theme. It is a gift I received many years ago from three friends.

The first friend is Henri J. M. Nouwen, a well-known theologian and author whose books, twenty years after his death, continue to inspire hundreds of thousands of people around the world.

The second friend is a mentor named Herb Cahoon,

whose memory lives on in the lives of the thousands of Yale students who at one point or another walked through his narrow office door.

My third friend is an El Salvadoran man with no known last name or date of birth. Unlike Henri Nouwen and Herb Cahoon, Alfredo died alone with no one to celebrate his life or mourn his death.

To the best of my knowledge, I was Alfredo's only friend. Perhaps for this reason, he taught me more about life and myself than I will ever fully know.

— • —

One of the most visible hats I wear is that of a fundraising consultant. As is true of most professions, a rather generic title like "fundraiser" tells you very little about who I am and what I actually do.

When someone first learns that I am a fundraiser, the conversation usually drifts off into a discussion of his or her work and occupation. Yet I do not see myself as a person who simply helps organizations raise money.

I am a person blessed with the desire and capacity to hear people's stories and help them build their dreams.

Several years ago, I started on a journey to share with the next generation of fundraisers what I have learned over the course of my 35-year career. This very ambitious venture began with a series of fifty short videos covering topics ranging from the importance of a donor pyramid to a series of techniques I have developed for identifying, cultivating, and soliciting large gifts of $100,000 or more.

One morning over coffee on the very last day of filming I realized that what I was presenting in my videos had very little to do with why I find great meaning and satisfaction in my work. Perhaps more important to other members of my profession, they also provide very little insight as to why I am successful at what I do.

At that point it came to me: What I really needed to share is the gift I received many years ago from three special friends. What follows are their stories.

Why stories? Early in life, you and I learned that telling and listening to stories is one of the primary ways that we, as people, connect with the world around us. The desire to tell a story and find someone who will listen is not simply an enjoyable experience. Telling and listening to stories are part of being human.

The story of a person who directly benefits from the work of an organization is obviously a very rich and deeply important story for a fundraiser to share. These are, in fact, the stories you hear repeated over and over in the fundraising letters that fill your mail box and, if successful, tug at both your heart and wallet.

For the purposes of fundraising (and many other professions), however, there is another place that is far more fertile ground for rich and powerful stories.

It is a place that most people rarely bother to look.

So where shall I begin? The most obvious place to start is with my own story.

1

The journey to El Salvador

"What *really matters* and what does not?"

In October of 1990, Earlham College, a liberal arts institution in Richmond, Indiana, successfully completed a $37 million capital campaign. With this campaign behind me, I informed Earlham's president that I was resigning as vice president for institutional advancement to spend a year living at an orphanage in El Salvador, a country I had visited numerous times and a people whose generous spirit I had grown to love.

To my surprise, my resignation was not accepted. Instead, I was graciously offered a year leave of absence. It was a response that said a lot about a small Quaker college that strives to live out its values and encourages faculty, staff, and students to do the same.

The decision to spend twelve months living with orphaned children in a country at war was not made

*I experienced the joy and privilege of being a human chair
with arms to wrap around children who did not have parents
to hold them.*

lightly. It was, however, a decision that fit very com-
fortably into my search for the answer to a very simple
question: *What, for me, really matters and what does not?*
Unlike the stereotypical man in his early forties seeking
adventure, I was not searching for excitement, nor was I
seeking an opportunity to abandon the rat race. Rather,
I was returning to my roots as a fundraiser who two
decades earlier was introduced to the profession by a
very unlikely person—a theologian named Henri J. M.
Nouwen, whom you will learn more about in the final

chapters of this book.

Not surprisingly, my decision to leave a rewarding career as a college vice president to go to El Salvador eventually took me away from the academic career path I had been trekking for some 20 years. My goal of climbing to the pinnacle of a college presidency faded. Over the next decade, of far more importance were the trips back and forth to El Salvador raising the money needed to enable more than 150 poor and orphaned children to attend school, help rebuild their country and seek new lives.

Listening with our hearts

Through my experiences in El Salvador, a new way of viewing the world began to unfold within me and become an increasingly powerful presence in my personal and professional life.

Many of the people who taught me what I needed to learn had absolutely nothing to put on their resume. Indeed, I learned some of my most important lessons from children whose whispers and giggles woke me up each morning as they climbed up and peeked over the plywood walls of my 6- by 10-foot "room" in the orphanage's outdoor laundry.

"Every day the helicopters would come
and shoot and bomb."
—14-year-old boy

While struggling to put pen to paper for this small book, I went through a stack of old boxes and found a bundle of children's drawings and a handful of letters I had sent to friends and family more than 20 years ago. Knowing that facts that were once fresh have a tendency to fade over time, I am relying on a few of these drawings and letters to share my story.

Given the reality of life in El Salvador, these pictures and letters were kept hidden until they could be smuggled out of the country. Most letters were delivered to a relative in the U.S. who then made copies that were sent to family, friends and colleagues. For security reasons, I did not identify the church I worked with or the location of the orphanage where I lived.

War through the eyes of a nine-year-old boy

"So there we sat, a man and a little boy."

I had been at the orphanage only a few short months when I wrote this letter to family and friends back in the States. Now, with the words of that letter again in

"I drew it because I remember it."
—Jose, 9 years old

front of me, my most vivid memory is of the moment Ricardo reached out and touched my hand, "palm-to-palm." That small gesture was an invitation—the kind we often experience but do not "see"—to be present with him as he was drawn back into a very painful time in his short life.

At that moment, there was nothing to say and nothing to do but sit beside him on our bus ride down the mountain.

Undated, 1991

Dear Friends,

There was nothing particularly special about Ricardo. In fact, I didn't even remember his name the day he grabbed my arm as we walked up the long hill to the bus that takes the children down the mountain each day to school.

Holding hands in the rough yet playful way that grown men and little boys often do, we walked along and talked about life at the orphanage and Ricardo's love of soccer. Indeed our very short conversation ended when he found a tin-can "soccer ball" and challenged the boys behind us to an impromptu game.

Having then turned my attention to the other children, I was surprised to find when I got to the bus that Ricardo had raced ahead and was saving a seat for me. Responding to his request, I sat down beside him and proceeded to learn more about this plain-looking little boy with dark eyes and a thin face. It was here that I learned that Ricardo was nine years old and had been at the orphanage for only six months.

As my new friend wrapped my big arm around his small shoulders, he began asking questions about why I talked funny, where I was from and why I decided to live with him and the other children at an orphanage in El Salvador. After briefly talking about why I was there, I told him that the reason I talked funny was that I was still learning Spanish. I then went on to explain that I was from the United States and not England, as he had guessed.

Putting his hand palm-to-palm against mine, Ricardo responded with a bombshell. "But the United States is bad. Their planes bombed us."

I was stunned. If Ricardo had yelled and pushed me away, I might have been able to offer some very superficial answer. In response, however, to the newly resurfaced memories of what happened to his family, this small innocent boy moved even closer, climbing into my lap in search of the security that one human being seeks in the warm body of another.

With his embrace, Ricardo left no room for anything but the truth about war—a truth found in the faces of its victims. It is a truth that can't be brushed aside with political arguments about defending freedom, "just" wars and national security. It is also a truth that can't be hidden from a nine-year-old boy who lives in an orphanage rather than with his family.

So there we sat—a 43-year-old North American man with tears in his eyes and a small Salvadoran boy with tears buried deep in his heart. Two of God's wounded children, a

man and a little boy, tenderly holding hands and comforting
each other.

Pushing away fear

One gift of childhood is the ability
to call other people away from their fears
and self-doubts.

At certain times, what we most fear is not the external danger we are facing but, rather, the dark inner place to which our fears and uncertainties take us. One of the gifts of childhood that we often lose as we grow older is the ability to call other people away from their fears and self-doubts. Through a child's simple desire and need for our presence, they invite us to take down our walls and join them in their world of hugs, games, and other simple experiences of childhood.

The following letter captures one of my darkest days in El Salvador. It also serves witness to the healing that often occurs when one person is authentically "there" for another person gripped by fear and self-doubt.

October 2, 1991

Dear Family,

At 2:30 yesterday afternoon, a man with an M-16 over his shoulder and hand grenades strapped to his waist got on the bus. His words were simple and to the point: "Everybody off."

In response to his command, I and the other men riding with me put our hands over our heads and lined up single file along the road at the rear of the bus. The women and children were segregated out and sent to the front.

When my turn came, I turned over my passport and leaned "spread-eagled" against the wire fence. To my left was a soldier dressed in a camouflage uniform with his finger on the trigger of his rifle. To my right were two more men in full army gear checking the spread-eagled passengers down the line.

Holding his rifle over his right shoulder, a soldier with a tattoo on his left arm crouched down behind me and used his free hand to feel around my ankles. Finding nothing, his hand moved up my body, between my legs, around my stomach and over my chest.

With a movement commanding me to turn around, the tattooed soldier looked with serious eyes at my passport. First page one, then two, three, four, and five. After checking page four for a second and third time, he gave it back to me.

"Thank you," I said.

He said nothing.

Another soldier, with a red bandana tied over his head, apparently had some questions for the young man beside me. A few whispered words were exchanged and a bribe went into the soldier's pocket.

After a few minutes, we heard the familiar "O.K." Having received our orders, I joined the other men, women and children filing back on the bus. We continued our journey in *silence.*

This was the fifth "everybody off" command I received this week: two times Monday, once Tuesday, a "rest day" on Wednesday, and twice today.

A heavy week—but it could have been worse. No one was taken away.

Reading again the words written last night I realize how much easier it is to talk about facts than it is to talk about fear.

While the details of the experience I have described are easy to remember, fear, powerlessness and degradation are feelings I try to push away, forget and not let get in my way.

The fact is that in El Salvador my world is controlled in many ways by the people who check my bags, feel my body and watch where I go. The control comes not from the fact that the soldiers have guns but rather from the fear and uncertainty that their power produces inside of me.

Life in El Salvador is a constant process of trying to predict what will happen next. What you carry in a bag, for example, is not determined solely by what you need to take from one place to another. Who may see it along the way is always a question. (In a country where hymn books are at times confiscated for being "subversive literature," letters such as this one are not casually carried around in one's back pocket.)

The control also exists at a deeper and much more disturbing level. It takes hold in the form of uncertainty about yourself and your actions. Most importantly, it enters your life in the form of questions that can be paralyzing:

What is wrong with me?

Why am I here?

Who can I trust?

For me, this deeper, more frightening level of control began to creep in following a particularly disturbing conversation one evening several weeks ago. It was during this conversation that I was told that men were seen earlier in the day writing down the license numbers of people entering the church. The pastor went on to express concern about several new people hanging around the church—people he believed to be "ears" sent to watch church members and monitor our activities. While not surprised by this news (which I had heard before), the conversation somehow moved me past the invisible line that separates "controlled concern" from the potentially paralyzing state of uncontrolled fear. All of a sudden, the experiences of other people—the disappearances, the arrests, and the threats received by church members—became a very real and frantic part of my life.

As I left the church that night and passed by the soldiers on my way back to the orphanage, I was overwhelmed by the need for something I could grab hold of, something in my life that made sense.

More than anything else, I wanted to fall asleep so I could wake up and find myself living a "normal life"—perhaps back at Earlham at a faculty meeting or talking over lunch with a donor. I wanted to be any place where I was away from the fear that was grabbing hold of me and taking me to some very frightening places in my imagination.

I spent that evening in bed curled up like a small child around a single lighted candle. I was alone in a way that

I have never been alone. Prayer, reflection, and imaginary conversations with far-off friends and family did not help.

The comfort that was not available to me that night arrived the next morning. It came in the form of children laughing.

As if the recipient of a marvelous gift, I woke up to the greeting of children who wanted to play—children who had stories to share, children who hugged me and asked that I hug them.

As I held Mimi, a five-year-old who seeks comfort each day in my overgrown North American lap, my doubts and fears began to slide away. Indeed, when I am with the children, all the big, fierce questions that haunt our adult lives seem far less important.

Having found a haven into which I can retreat, I now set aside time each day to sit quietly in a corner waiting for any child who wants to join me. In a place filled with children who have lost their families, I am not alone very long. Within minutes my lap is filled with children who need someone to hug, children who seem to recognize that this is a special time set aside for renewal rather than play.

For anywhere from a few minutes to an hour, we sit quietly—as quietly as little children can sit. They show me cut fingers, little pieces of string, and places where they have bumped their head.

I nod, say nothing, and hug them.

During the brief time we share, the world—for me and for the children—is a better place. It is a place far removed from the war that surrounds us.

— • —

With a population of approximately five million people, El Salvador is the smallest and most densely populated country in Central America. This letter was written in the final months of a twelve-year civil war that took, by some estimates, 75,000 civilian lives.

Throughout my time in El Salvador, I was often told that bad things were less likely to happen if a North American's "eyes" were present. At times, soldiers would come onto the bus and then leave when they saw my blond hair or heard my very poor Spanish.

One of the primary forms of military recruitment was to set up checkpoints, stop buses and take young men away. I witnessed this abduction and forced recruitment an average of once or twice per week.

2

Confessions
of good deeds

There is only one way out of fear
and that is love.

—William Sloane Coffin

When we fear another person, it is very easy for
our fear to distort our view of that person and the world
around us. Often, the line between fear and hate dis-
solves, leaving us caught in an endless cycle where fear
breeds hate and hate breeds fear, both in ourselves and
in others.

El Salvador in the early 1990s was, without question, a place where it was easy to fear and hate another
person. It was also a place where I met a woman gifted
with the ability to find good in others, including those
she had every reason to fear and distrust.

Sister Margaret was a 66-year-old Franciscan nun
from the United States. A very small woman with a
quiet voice and gentle manner, Sister Margaret and I

18

spent many hours together both in deep conversation and sharing moments of laughter. Over the course of several months, she became a good friend who taught me many lessons about how to find the good that resides in all of us.

One of the most important lessons I learned from Sister Margaret came about one morning as we were walking together down a busy street in San Salvador, the nation's capital. With buses and cars noisily rushing by, our conversation stopped when, up ahead, I saw a line of soldiers walking in our direction. As I'd so often observed, their faces were frozen into tight masks, betraying no emotion as they marched single file toward us with guns drawn and fingers held close to the trigger. While most looked directly forward, others scanned the street and alleyways, anticipating whatever danger might cross their path.

From the first day I arrived in El Salvador, I learned that soldiers would be an ever-present part of my life. At the same time, I learned from the children that the soldiers were supposed to be invisible. They were people whom you responded to when they spoke but whom you otherwise tried not to "see." When in the presence of a soldier, all conversation stopped and people stood still, silently waiting for what would happen next. Very simply put, if the soldiers were invisible to you perhaps in some magical way you would be invisible to them.

Sister Margaret, however, approached the world differently. On that morning as I turned my eyes away, Sister Margaret stopped still and confronted each soldier with a big smile and warm greeting. "Good morning," she said to each of the twelve young men as they passed by.

"Good morning. . . . Good morning. . . . Good morning," she repeated to each one.

Soldier after soldier ignored her. Then, for reasons unknown, one soldier halfway down the line acknowledged Sister Margaret's greeting with a slight nod of his head. Moments later, two soldiers behind him offered two very quiet "good mornings."

Having witnessed this brief exchange between Sister Margaret and the soldiers, I told her how moved I was to see the response of the three young men who had ever-so-faintly acknowledged her greeting. She then shared a story with me that opened my eyes to a new way of seeing people I fear.

Sister Margaret's days in El Salvador were primarily spent in the countryside where many people—especially children—die each year from malnutrition and disease. The primary focus of her work was helping train "foot doctors," primarily older, well-respected women in the community who would learn about nutrition, sanitation, and the use of local remedies to treat children and families who did not have access to prescription drugs or modern-day medical care.

In El Salvador, this was dangerous work. Healthcare workers of any sort were often viewed as aiding the rebels, especially if they were working in a "conflicted zone" where the military and rebel forces often fought for control of an area or village.

One day while in a small rural village, Sister Margaret found herself sitting alone with an hour to spare as she waited to assist with the training of several foot doctors from the community. Being Sister Margaret, she became engaged in playful conversation with some of the children and their mothers as they passed by. When one of the mothers asked what she was doing, Sister Margaret spontaneously announced that she was there to hear "confessions of good deeds." She went on to explain that she was a Franciscan nun who found great joy in hearing people say something good about themselves. In her words, "If you need to confess your sins, go to your priest. I am here to hear confessions of good deeds! Tell me something good you have done with your life."

Soon, with a mother's urging, a shy boy came forward and "confessed" that every morning he helped his father pick the beans they then sold to feed their family. He went on to explain that he was *very good* at picking beans—faster than many boys twice his age! After confirming the good deeds of her son, this proud mother then brought forward her daughter who exclaimed with great pride that she was only six but already knew how to make tortillas!

As people learned about Sister Margaret's desire to hear their confessions of good deeds, a small line soon formed. One by one, women and children waited their turn to share something they were proud of about themselves—some small way in which they found meaning in their lives, their role in their family, and their life as part of their community.

The line soon brought the attention of two soldiers who, up until that point, had watched from a distance. As they grew more curious the soldiers, both of whom were young men in their late teens or early twenties, approached Sister Margaret and asked what she was doing. When she explained that she was hearing confessions of good deeds, one of the soldiers laughed at what he clearly viewed to be a silly old woman. He walked away.

As Sister Margaret listened to the next person in

Soldiers on the steps of a church in El Salvador.
Chris Steele Perkins, Magnum Photos.

line, she noticed that the other soldier stood about fifteen feet away, watching her silently and very intently.
In his eyes she saw the spark of a person who had something to say—perhaps something to share.

After several minutes, Sister Margaret motioned
to the soldier and with a wave of her hand invited him
to come over. Reluctantly, the young man walked over
and stood beside her. Sister Margaret smiled and asked
him to share with her a good deed: "Something about
yourself that you are proud of. Something you feel very
good about."

With a sheepish smile, the young soldier confessed that he had *nothing* good to say about himself. When Sister Margaret's eyes told him that we all have something that is good within us, he stood still and seemed to search thoughtfully for a few words to share. After a moment, he leaned in close so he could tell her something he did not want anyone else to hear.

"I have never intentionally hurt anyone," he whispered.

Sister Margaret reached out, touched his hand, and thanked him for his confession. After a few silent moments the soldier walked away.

—   •   —

Could this soldier be one of the many young men I saw taken off a bus and forced into the military? Or, could he be a young man who volunteered to serve believing he was protecting his family from evil people who were out to destroy his country? He certainly could have been one of the soldiers who frequently stopped me late at night to check my passport—a person I feared as we stood alone, him with a rifle and me fearful of what he might do to me in the darkness of night.

From that day forward, I realized that one of the first causalities of our fear is the ability to see glimpses of the good that resides in every human being, including those we have reason to fear and distrust.

From that day forward, I followed Sister Margaret's example of acknowledging each soldier as he walked by with a slight nod of my head or a simple greeting. Each of these small acts of greeting empowered me to take control of my fear. By acknowledging the humanity of each soldier, I experienced an inner strength guns and power could not provide.

3

A mother and child by the side of the road

Happiness is often found when our search for it is abandoned.

Stripped of our outer trappings, we were simply two parents sharing in the pain that comes with loving our children. This is a moment and memory I often return to when I see a mother and child holding hands and walking together.

May 14, 1992

Dear Friends and Family,

Yesterday was a day that began like many others. It ended, however, with fresh memories of a mother and child facing life and death on the side of a road waiting for a bus to take them to the place they call home.

The story began as I was driving along in a borrowed truck down the mountain from the orphanage to the church. Rounding a bend several blocks from my destination, I noticed a small woman on the other side of the road carrying with some difficulty a young boy almost half her size.

Like dangling pieces of rope, the child's arms and legs swayed in rhythm to each of the woman's small, cautious steps. Even at a distance, I could tell that these were not the arms and legs of a boy who merely sought rest and comfort in the arms of his mother.

Passing by these two lone figures, I went to the church and picked up the papers required for my upcoming visit to Guatemala. As I had expected, when I came around the curve on my return trip the woman was still standing on the side of the road holding her child, his thin arms and legs hanging limply by her side.

I continued down the road only to find myself at the next corner turning around and asking the woman if she wanted a ride. Her answer provides insight as to how she, a poverty-stricken woman in a Third World country, might view the Good Samaritan story:

"But sir, I don't have any money. I cannot pay you."

In my limited Spanish, I convinced the woman that money wasn't necessary. Then, with some reluctance and a bewildered look, she lifted both herself and her child off the pavement and onto the seat beside me.

Not knowing what to do, I drove down the road with no idea where either she or I were heading. Clearly, however, we had both ventured into new territory that until that moment had separated our two worlds.

Perhaps knowing the question that lingered just out of my reach, the woman told me that her ten-year-old son was very sick. In response to my question as to where she lived, she replied with an unknown name and the clarification that home was "Very far away. Two hours by bus."

In the minutes that followed, we fumbled our way through a discussion about the cost of medicine (ten colones, or roughly $1.25) and where she could catch a bus that would take her out of the city back to her home in the countryside.

Reaching into my pocket I gave my new passenger what for me would buy a nice meal but to her would probably equal a week's income. Realizing that this was an awkward moment, I bridged the silence by explaining that I, too, had children who needed medicine when they were sick.

The smile that greeted me was the smile of a mother who realized that in her young son I saw my own children when, years earlier, I yearned to heal bruises and brush away tears of pain. Across our cultural boundaries we shared the role of parent—protectors of the next generation, breadwinners for our families. Nothing else needed to be said.

As the woman got out of the truck at the bus stop, my initial fears returned. The small arm that fell from a mother's grasp onto the seat beside me showed no sign of life. Watching the arm's inert path as it was dragged across the seat, I realized that we, as parents, were too late.

The boy was dead.

With only a few weeks left before I return to the United States, I find myself waking up at night thinking about the culture shock that lies ahead. Most of my time during the past 12 months has been filled with a wide array of human emotions. With the ups and downs of a roller coaster, I have witnessed both the pain of intense poverty and the personal joy of realizing that much of what I have I don't really need.

Perhaps most important of all, I have learned that happiness is found when our search for it is abandoned. Indeed, for most of us, happiness sits on the other side of our walls waiting patiently for us to open our doors to the joy and pain of the world around us.

4

Seeing relationships through a different lens

"Perhaps how we view others determines how they view us."

The transition back to the United States from El Salvador was not easy, especially as I returned to my professional life as a fundraiser.

The story presented below provides a brief window into how relationships are understood and experienced in different cultural and organizational settings.

Several years ago in a conversation with a new client, I asked the school's most experienced fundraiser to tell me about a very generous donor he and others had described as being "deeply connected" to their school. In answer, this veteran fundraiser turned to a pile of research about the donor and cited the couple's financial resources, the value of their home and their engagement in various charitable activities in the community.

This fundraiser also reported a detailed list of events the donor had attended, notes from visits with the donor in his home and a record of gifts received over the past 15 years. Personal information included that the couple always designated their gifts to support scholarships; that they had three children (and two grandchildren); and the fact that they "just loved" the school.

This kind of conversation in the business world is by no means unique. And, as a fundraising consultant, it is a window into how many people in my profession respond when I ask them to tell me about a donor.

This fundraiser's immediate focus on quantifiable "facts" and research "about" the donor tells me a lot about how he sees this person as a potential source of financial support. But it tells me virtually *nothing* about how this person views himself *behind* all of the images, numbers and facts that the school—and society—use to label and describe him.

That, to me, is very sad for everyone involved. It is particularly sad for the person whose life has been summed up by a series of labels and "facts" that reflect only a small portion of who he is.

In the first few pages of this book, I shared with you *very little* about myself in a traditional sense. You can, however, go to my website and get a bucket full of factual information about me as a consultant, my degrees, and the clients I serve. You also, I am sure, can use a wealth search engine to find out about my financial capacity and income level, the value of my house, my wife's name and the names and ages of our children and grandchildren.

Out of all the information you were able to gather, what would be the most helpful in terms of knowing who I am and the person I see in the mirror each morning? Was it what is available on-line and through your research? Or, is it the "window" into my life that I shared with you through three letters and two children's drawings?

The sad truth is that many people in my profession (and, most likely, yours) never move beyond the facts they have gathered in how they see the people with whom they believe they have a meaningful relationship. Equally important, most professional work environments are organized around seeing people through the lens of what we know *about the person* rather than the lens through which the person sees him or her self.

Is it any wonder that some members of my profession find it difficult to get people to meet with them?

Perhaps how we view a person determines how they view us?

5

Steak and asparagus with Margaret

"What is it, Henry, that you want
to talk about?"

A number of years ago when I was vice president
at Earlham, I had a visit with someone who showed me
what it means to be in an authentic relationship with
another person. Earlham was in the middle of a capital
campaign and I had just completed a hectic month of
travel. After a few days back in the office I was again on
the road for a two-day East Coast trip.

My trip started out with an all-day meeting in New
Haven, Connecticut followed by dinner that evening
in Hartford with a donor. My plan was to then make a
late-night, three-hour drive to Boston for an important
breakfast meeting with a group of campaign volunteers.
I was packing a lot into a very short time period, each of
these meetings was important in its own way and, from
my perspective, nothing on my agenda could be left out.

The trip started badly. While my plane arrived on time the night before, the all-day meeting at Yale went on two-hours longer than I had planned for. Adding to my anxiety and frustration was a traffic jam on the drive to Hartford that kept me at a standstill for more than an hour.

As this was long before the era of cell phones and texting, I could not call ahead to explain my dilemma to the Hartford donor. Instead, I began to calculate in my head what I could do to remain on schedule. The answer was clear: If I could limit our dinner to one hour, I would still be able to get a few hours of sleep before my breakfast meeting in Boston the following morning.

While I viewed the dinner meeting in Hartford as important for growing my relationship with this particular donor, I knew it would not lead to a significant gift to the campaign. My host was an elderly woman who had been generous to Earlham in years past and had been very open about telling me that the college was in her estate for $60,000. During our last visit, however, Margaret had declined to entertain a request that she establish a one-million dollar endowment for student scholarships.

Our research showed that she was clearly capable of such a gift and we knew from an earlier conversation that her accountant agreed that such a gift was feasible. But Margaret was haunted by memories of her poverty-stricken childhood during the Depression. When I asked for the gift, she told me that she very much wanted to support Earlham but that she was fearful of giving away money that she may need at some future point to buy groceries.

While the fundraiser in me knew that a conversation about a planned gift in her estate was an obvious next step that was not the purpose of this dinner. My goal was simply that of "keeping in touch" in a way that might open the door for a future conversation about her estate plans.

As I reached the front gate of the retirement community, I decided I would make a point of mentioning early in our visit that I had run into problems with traffic. I would also apologize for the fact that I needed to leave a bit early because I had already booked my hotel room in Boston and had a 7 AM meeting the next morning.

From the moment this small gentle woman greeted me at her door, my plans were shot. After a brief hug and hello, Margaret asked the question that she said had been on her mind all day.

"Henry, now be honest with me. Do you like fresh asparagus? If you don't I have some frozen carrots in the freezer that are also very, very good."

After I confirmed with a smile that I absolutely love asparagus—a slight exaggeration but an essentially truthful response—she asked how I like my steak. She then explained that she had ordered Omaha Steaks in preparation for my visit but wanted to be sure that she cooked them "just right."

Over the next hour, we made small talk as I sat at the dining room table and she stood at her stove cooking our steaks and asparagus. Before I could explain why I was late and why I might need to leave a bit early, she said she had been worried about me.

"Henry, you travel so much. What would happen if you were in an accident? I had hoped that nothing was wrong or perhaps that you had just forgotten about our plans."

Now long past when I had hoped dinner would be over, my host brought to our small table a plate of asparagus and two plates with a tasty, medium-cooked Omaha Steak for each of us. Before digging into our meal she asked if I would join her for a moment of silence, which is the Quaker-inspired form of prayer that alumni often suggest when I meet with them.

For the next few moments I waited for my host to break the silence. Finally, she uttered these words,

"Thank you, God, for having Henry here so I have some-one to talk to."

Knowing that I had just been invited into an import-ant moment in another person's life, I looked across the table at a small frail woman with tears in her eyes.

"What is it, Margaret, that you would like to talk with me about?"

Margaret then told me that she'd learned earlier in the day that she was dying of cancer. Having ventured out from behind her protective wall into a very scary place, she then withdrew with a question for me.

"What is it, Henry, that *you* want to talk about?"

During a few more moments of silence, I struggled with how to respond. Knowing that I was about to begin a very special journey with her, I told Margaret about the mood I was in and the fact that I had arrived at her door with every intention of leaving as soon as I could. I then apologized for entering her life in a way that no human being should ever do.

"You, Margaret, had invited me into your home and your life as a guest," I said. "I, however, did not arrive as a guest. I arrived this evening as a person with an agenda and you were part of that agenda. And that is not appropriate nor is it fair."

Then I said, "The real agenda is to talk about what

is important in your life."

For the next three hours, Margaret and I sat together as she unfolded her memories of childhood and people who were important to her. At times the stories brought laughter and at other times, tears. She then talked about her fear of a painful death.

Her desire, she said, was to simply fall asleep.

At the end of our time together, I thanked Margaret for giving me a gift I hope I never forget. The gift I received that night was the knowledge that I was a guest in her home and that I need to always be ready to leave my agenda at the door when invited into the life of another person. More importantly, I need to always make space for what is in the heart of the people who welcome me into their lives.

That night I arrived at my hotel in Boston at about two AM. I then had my seven AM meeting and flew back to Indiana later that day.

A month later I arranged a trip back to Hartford to visit with Margaret. In a phone conversation with her the week before, she asked that I call her when I arrived at the airport. When I got into the terminal and placed the call, I was surprised to hear an unfamiliar female voice on the other end of the phone. "Yes, Margaret is resting, but she is looking forward to seeing you."

After renting a car, I made the 45-minute journey to see Margaret. When I arrived I didn't need to knock on her door. It was open. A housekeeper was cleaning.

Margaret had died shortly before my arrival.

—   •   —

The evening I joined Margaret for our dinner of Omaha steak and asparagus, I entered her apartment with all of my research in order and knowing everything about her that someone in my profession needs to know. I wore the hat of a fundraiser and the financial agenda that goes with the title.

When entering the life of another person, the problem is not that we are tired, wear a particular professional hat or bring along an agenda as we knock on the door. The problem is that so often we ignore the small inner voice that invites us to take off our professional hat and put our agenda aside.

6

Alfredo, my friend and teacher

"We need friends.
Friends guide us,
care for us,
confront us in love,
console us in times of pain."

—Henri J. M. Nouwen

Fundraising is a profession that centers on the ability of people to give money. But does this mean that fundraising has to be a distasteful activity obsessively focused on a person's wealth and financial circumstances?

This has not been the case for me, nor has it been the experience of most of my clients. In fact, the deepest and most powerful experiences I have had as a fundraiser have occurred after the curtain we call "wealth" has been lifted. It's at the point when I have the privilege of being invited behind a person's financial bottom line that many of my deepest and most meaningful relationships unfold.

So, who is a wealthy person once we see the individual "behind" their money? My friend, Alfredo, shared the answer with me.

— • —

In 1994, two years after I returned to the United States, a man with clubbed feet and a deteriorating body died on the streets of El Salvador. To me and the many others who watched his body rot away and his spirit snuffed out by disease and poverty, his name was simply Alfredo.

To most people, Alfredo was a nameless and pathetic figure whose crippled body could often be seen lying across the sidewalk asleep two blocks from the president's mansion—El Salvador's "White House." To me, however, Alfredo was a friend—a person whose losing struggle to remain part of the human race taught me what it means to connect with another person and be invited into his or her life story.

In 1991 and 1992, conversations with Alfredo became part of my daily life as I passed by him each morning on my way to and from the orphanage. When Alfredo and I talked, it was usually in response to an outstretched hand that connected me to a man who

Alfredo.

would not let go. Gradually, with each passing day, he became a friend who eagerly invited me to sit down beside him and respond to his one and only question.

He would ask, "How are you, my brother?"

I would reply, "I am well. And you?"

Alfredo would simply laugh and give me a big hug. Then, a few minutes later he would repeat his question, "How are you, my brother?"

And I would respond with the same answer again. And again. And again.

Our friendship was based on nothing more than

Alfredo's single question and the simple act of sitting together with an arm around each other's shoulder. Except for the ability—and willingness—to touch each other, there was little else we could share. (If I asked Alfredo a direct question about his life, his only response was a burst of laughter.)

When I first got to know Alfredo, he was a crippled man with a broad grin and spontaneous laugh. He was an easy man to be with because his smile reflected light within his pitifully broken body. After several months, however, Alfredo's smile faded as his body gradually became a living bed of sores and rotting flesh. Surrounded by flies, he became the most grotesque-looking human being I had ever seen.

Over time, as Alfredo declined, I had trouble catching my breath when close to him. Still, we sat together and, when I could, I would hold his hand or touch a place on his arm that was free of sores or broken flesh. He, in turn, would put his arm around my shoulder or, on some of his most difficult days, find the strength to rest the palm of his hand on my knee.

Our time together was no longer something I felt good about or looked forward to. Some days, I would see Alfredo from a distance and intentionally take another route in order to avoid him. Touching Alfredo had become a *duty* I felt deep inside—an obligation grounded in the fact that if I didn't touch my friend, something in him would die. Or, perhaps, my real fear was that something within me—something I had grown to value and treasure—would be lost.

My ability to continue to touch Alfredo was also grounded in the question he *always* asked regardless of his condition.

"How are you, my brother?"

I would reply, as always, "I am well. And you?

The good samaritans

One morning as I was headed down the road to sit with Alfredo, I noticed two well-dressed women walking toward us from the other end of the street. Even from a distance I could see in their faces the pity and alarm they felt when they saw Alfredo lying in their path twenty feet ahead. Startled and repelled by my friend's crippled body and open sores, the two ladies cautiously crossed to the other side of the street where they searched their bags for whatever coins they could find. After gathering together a hand full of loose change, the taller of the two women tossed the coins as far as she could in Alfredo's direction. Disappointed that most of the coins had fallen far short of their mark, she then loudly exclaimed, "This is for food!"

Still a half block away, I stood motionless as I watched my friend search for a way to collect the coins. With each painful movement, Alfredo slowly crawled on his hands and knees to the gutter fresh with water from a morning rain where most of the coins had landed. Then, still motionless, I stared as my friend retrieved from the muddy puddle of water each of the coins the two ladies had thrown to him so that he could buy food.

As I watched this modern-day version of the Good Samaritan Story unfold I learned *why* I needed to touch Alfredo. I came to understand in that moment that being *part of my friend's life* added *wholeness* to my own. To abandon my contact with Alfredo would be to abandon a very special person—a human being who asked nothing of me but to be his friend. Distancing myself from Alfredo would also have required that I turn my back on something within me that Alfredo had helped me find.

Something we, as human beings, can *feel* and *experience* but few of us can express in words.

Saying goodbye

Through some miracle I still cannot fathom, over

the next few months Alfredo's health began to improve. By the time I left El Salvador in June 1992 (the day I took the photograph used in this book), life was back in my friend's eyes.

On the final day before I returned to the States, Alfredo and I sat together and exchanged farewells. With our arms wrapped around each other's shoulders, I promised him that I would come back for a visit. (I was able to honor that commitment on three subsequent trips.)

On my fourth trip back to El Salvador I went in search of my friend. Not finding him at his usual place on the corner, I asked the owner of a small store nearby where I could find Alfredo.

"He died," the man said. Like a bag of trash, Alfredo's body had been picked up and hauled away.

Twenty years later, I still miss Alfredo. As I look at his picture, the memory that comes to mind is of Alfredo's outstretched hands—hands that to most people belonged to a beggar asking for their money. To me, however, they were an invitation—the gesture of a man who invited me to sit down beside him and be part of his life.

Words of wisdom from an unlikely teacher

"Sometimes our concern for the poor may carry with it a prejudice against the rich."
—Henri J. M. Nouwen

So, what words of wisdom might Alfredo share with us about our wealth and personal circumstances? What would this man with no public voice and no schooling say if he were invited to speak to a class at Indiana's Lilly Family School of Philanthropy or in a lecture hall at a professional fundraiser's conference?

Nervously standing at the podium, Alfredo might begin his remarks by expressing his appreciation for the coins we so often throw from a distance that enable him to buy food. But when he looked out into the audience, he would search for signs that he was more than a stage prop representing the world's poor.

If in our faces he found people who truly wanted to know *him* as a person, he would repeat back to us what deep down we already know:

> "The most important gift you can give me is to see me as a human being who, like you, has a story to share but few people who will listen."

Perhaps Alfredo would also quote another gifted teacher and friend of mine:

> "The roots of loneliness are very deep and cannot be touched by optimistic advertisements, substitute love images or social togetherness. They find their food in the suspicion that there is no one who cares and offers love without conditions, and no place where we can be vulnerable without being used."
>
> —Henri J. M. Nouwen

7

A space to be vulnerable

A gift from Henri Nouwen

A space to be vulnerable is not a gift
    we can learn or acquire with our head.
It is a gift that only exists when shared
    heart-to-heart with another.

On most of our journeys through life there is a thread that weaves together what appear to be distinctly separate places of rest along the way. For me, that thread is a gift I received from Henri Nouwen.

Henri Nouwen shared his gift with me as I sat in my first and only class with him at Yale Divinity School. The year was 1973 and, while more than forty years have passed, the memory is still fresh in my mind. It was a transformational moment, a point in time when my life was altered and a new journey began.

Sitting in the second row, I listened as this wise professor in his early 40s spent the next hour inviting his students into conversation about what it meant to genuinely and authentically be present with another person. That was it. That was all he asked us to do.

It was clear that Professor Nouwen was not interested in the class coming up with a sophisticated and complicated answer. In this class, a language of the heart was spoken. All the head stuff—the theories we could learn from books—was of no interest to him.

In Henri Nouwen's class a space opened up for me to explore something that throughout my life has made me feel different from other people in a frustrating and, at times, embarrassing way. Something that, over time, I have come to believe is a gift I have received rather than a burden I must bear.

My secret

In Professor Nouwen's class and every other class at Yale, there were many bright students with degrees from prestigious schools and high grade-point averages. In this class, there was also at least one student who came to Yale committed to keeping part of his life secret.

That student was me. I was a young 23-year-old who had made it to Yale from Rock Hill, South Carolina for one simple reason. I tried very, very hard and overcame—with a lot of listening in class and very intense study—a major obstacle along the way.

Henri Nouwen with children in Santiago Atitlan,
Guatemala (1984).
Photo by Peter Weiskel; used by permission.

To this day, I love to read and take in the feelings and stories that are found in a good novel or the
wisdom recorded in the pages of a scholar's book. The
problem is that 24 hours later I am left with only the
vaguest memory of what I read one day earlier. Not the
name of the author, the story or the plot—nothing that
stays in my head from the written words alone. What I
can remember (and often in great detail) is the book I
have turned into a story and shared with myself through
a conversation in my head, an interesting discussion
with another person or a speech to an invisible audience
behind my bathroom mirror.

While I have learned various ways to translate written words into stories and voices—both my own and others—it is a tiring, stressful and time-consuming process. For this reason, school—and certainly being at Yale—was a time of great stress interwoven with the joy I experience when exploring ideas and learning new things through my interactions with other people.

In Professor Nouwen's class I found, for the first time in my life, a kindred spirit—a person who also experienced the world as I do. Not as volumes of information surrounded by complicated words but through simple questions about small moments in an ordinary person's life.

In that hour Henri Nouwen opened my eyes to the possibility that my difficulty with reading might be a special gift. I began to view my handicap as a small window into a world that is not cluttered by words on paper. And, I came to understand why I have always experienced the world less through a world of facts and more through a world of feelings.

The gift I received from Henri Nouwen over four decades ago was what I now describe as a *space to be vulnerable.*

It is a space where at various points on my life journey I return and, metaphorically speaking, sit in Henri

Nouwen's class again and experience the same vulnerability and acceptance I found that day.

It is a space I returned to twenty years later and found the strength to tell Earlham's president and members of the faculty that I was leaving to live in the laundry of an orphanage in El Salvador. Something college vice presidents just don't do unless your teacher was Henri Nouwen, who left Yale years earlier to be with and learn from street children in Latin America.

It is a space where I found another teacher in Alfredo, a homeless man that the world would say had nothing to teach me.

It is a space where Alfredo and I were both vulnerable—two people from two different worlds being present for each other and enjoying their time together.

Alfredo's corner of a sidewalk in El Salvador was a space where I was *at home*. Perhaps I felt as Henri did when, in the last decade of his life, he found a home living at L'Arche Community in Toronto, Canada, where he shared his life with a mentally-challenged man named Adam.

Like Alfredo, Adam was a wise teacher who could not read the words in Henri's books but could read the words in his friend's heart.

But there is another gift I received from Henri

Nouwen that day. It is the gift of understanding what it means to be a fundraiser.

The gift of being a fundraiser

A space to be vulnerable is a gift one person experiences with another then shares with someone else.

As I sat in class listening to Henri Nouwen explore what it means to be present with another person, I struggled for the courage to go through with my plan to drop his seminar and leave Yale to do something I had no experience doing but I knew I had to do.

Several months earlier I had seen a picture of a small girl at a rehabilitation center in Vietnam that made artificial legs for children wounded in the Vietnam War. This small girl with beautiful big eyes needed a pair of artificial legs and the Quang Ngai Rehabilitation Center needed $500,000 to remain open.

For weeks it had been crystal clear to me: I needed to raise $500,000 so that children in Vietnam could walk again. I didn't know how I was going to do it, but that was what I was going to do.

It was a very simple challenge when seen through the eyes of a 23-year-old with absolutely no fundraising experience. It was also a calling that would be perceived as naïve by many people. To others, including several of my classmates, it was simply a stupid idea stuck in the head of someone who had arrived at Yale from a small town in South Carolina.

But this was not the view of Henri Nouwen, a man who also saw the world through small, vulnerable places where eyes connect and God is at work.

To Henri, I was a young person who needed to stay at Yale and remain in his class. With these two goals in mind, he made a phone call to Dwight Hall to see if they were still looking for a student who needed a job in order to pay his tuition.

But Professor Nouwen did more. He also saw in me a fundraiser who had said he needed $135 so he could establish The Student Fund for Vietnamese Children, an organization that was nothing more than the dream of a young person who couldn't let go of the story he saw in the eyes of a Vietnamese girl with no legs.

That night after I went to bed, an envelope was slipped under my door. No note, just an envelope with $135 in cash.

That $135 was more than my first fundraising donation. It was a gift from Henri Nouwen that said, simply, "I believe in you."

I was captivated by the eyes of a small girl
with no legs.

For the next eight years I remained at Yale—first as
a student, and then for the last three years as Executive
Director of Dwight Hall, an organization and campus
ministry best described as the center for volunteerism
and social action at Yale. Throughout those eight years,
Henri and I would occasionally chat. Most of the time
our contact was through an occasional wave or a short
conversation as each of us walked by.

Henri, however, had not abandoned me.

With his call to Dwight Hall in 1973, Henri gently
opened another door behind which he introduced me

to Yale's director of volunteer services, Herb Cahoon.

Like Henri, Herb Cahoon experienced the world through small windows into the lives of other people. He was a man as comfortable with the homeless people he frequently sat with on the streets of New Haven as he was behind the closed door of his office with a Yale student trying to find his way out from under a famous last name or the expectations of a wealthy family.

Or, in my case, a young divinity school student who needed help along his journey to raise $500,000 so that a small Vietnamese girl with big, beautiful eyes could walk.

8

Herbert A. Cahoon and Mary

Every year like clockwork,
"Old Man Cahoon" called.

When I walked through the doors of Dwight Hall, the first person I met was a short "old guy" in his mid-fifties with a smelly, ugly pipe lazily hanging from the corner of his mouth. In the eyes of everyone who knew him, Herbert A. Cahoon was a real character. He was also a "cantankerous friend" from the first time he met you. As my toddler-aged twins soon learned, Herb was a "funny old man" who would show up at a child's birthday party at the invitation of a two-year old. (He was also the same "Herbie" who called on David and Sara's birthday for each of the next twenty-eight years. It didn't matter where they were; old man Cahoon would track them down, sing Happy Birthday at the top of his lungs, learn about their lives, hang up and then call again the next year!)

Working within the ivy-covered halls of Yale, Herb cared little about the intellectual capacity of the people he met. What he cared about was each and every person in front of him at that specific point in time. A person's strengths and weaknesses simply came as part of the luggage each person carried with them when they walked up the stairs to Herb's unassuming office on the second floor of Dwight Hall.

When dealing with Yale students, Herb could be both an encouraging father and a harsh critic. One of his greatest gifts was the ability to see in people a dream that could change the world. It didn't matter how idealistic the dream, Herb would make it appear to be rational and doable. In turn, when dealing with a Yale student who saw himself as better than other people, Herb had a way of gently laughing in his face and bringing him back to reality.

One day, I remember Herb facing down a boastful Yale student with the comment, "Well I'll be. Another very smart Yalie with the entire world at his finger tips! I am *so impressed!*" Within the next hour Herb would have that same Yale student tutoring a child in inner-city New Haven, sharing a meal at the Community Soup Kitchen, or volunteering with one of the twenty other programs

Herb and Jean Cahoon.
Used with permission of the Cahoon family.

that operated under the Dwight Hall umbrella.

More importantly, the student would leave Dwight Hall knowing that Herb both valued and respected the human being who lived behind the emotional and psychological walls that so many of us erect to protect ourselves and keep others out. Once a Yale student knew that about Herb, they found in him space where simply being "me" was both comfortable and welcomed.

Herb's approach to life didn't fit with the way my 23-year-old self expected the world to be. For much of my time at Yale, I was like most young adults in their first real job starting off life's journey on a road with only one end in mind. I wanted to *be somebody,* and working at Yale felt like a pretty good place to start.

A good portion of my first few years as a work-study student at Dwight Hall were spent thinking that what I was doing and accomplishing was important. What I soon learned from Herb was that my role at Dwight Hall was not to accomplish something, but to nurture the accomplishments and dreams of others. For Herb, it wasn't the size of the vision or dream. It was the fact that someone *had* a vision or dream.

For every highly successful student who benefited from their relationship with Herb Cahoon, there was someone else whose life had taken a different turn. Herb was at home with virtually everyone, ranging from a homeless person who slept on the streets of New Haven to members of the Yale Corporation.

There was one very special relationship that reflects Herb's qualities and character more so than any other. The relationship was with a woman named Mary.

— • —

"We are going to sit down and talk."

When I first met Mary, she was standing silently in the corner of Dwight Hall's outer office where students frequently gathered to plan new projects, organize a student protest, or simply hang out and talk. As students walked by, Mary nervously stared at the ceiling while talking to herself and murmuring a string of words that made no sense.

Mary was a woman totally out of touch with the world. The only rational decision she was able to make was to put one foot in front of the other and make her way to Dwight Hall and ask to see Herb.

Mary was a person who needed help finding the woman trapped in the body of a homeless bag lady. The only person who could see the person behind Mary's panicked eyes was Herb Cahoon. With one quick phone call up to his office, Herb was in front of Mary staring into her eyes and telling her what she needed to know.

"Mary, you are doing it again. You are making no sense. We are going to sit down and talk."

Right there with students walking back and forth, Herb and Mary shared a space that no one else was privileged to enter. From the door of my office I watched as he gently coaxed from Mary a short string of words that were understandable. Gradually, over the next hour, the conversation moved from gibberish to a genuine dialogue between two people. One person was confused and imprisoned in the scary world around her and the other was willing to be present in that scary world with her.

When Mary walked out of Dwight Hall that day, she was still a bag lady whose day-to-day life would never change. A psychiatrist might even say that Mary left the outer office of Dwight Hall no better off than when she came in.

Mary did, however, have in Herb Cahoon someone who was willing and able to be present with her for that hour of her life.

Over the years, Mary showed up at Dwight Hall many, many times. Each time, Herb was there for her.

As far as I know, Herb was never too busy to see Mary—a person who sheltered a special place in her life that only he was allowed to enter.

9

Learning to fail

Serving soup and building dreams

"My name is Henry and your name is
Henry. . . . So we are like brothers. Right?"

My guess is that Herb knew from the day I walked through Dwight Hall's front door that my plan to raise $500,000 was a very ambitious dream that would fail. Why would students at colleges around the country organize local chapters of The Student Fund for Vietnamese Children simply because they received a letter from a divinity student at Yale who asked them to organize around his dream and send him a check? My guess is that Henri Nouwen also smiled when I told him that his $135 was going to buy nothing more than stamps for a letter to each student government office at 1,000 colleges and universities around the country.

But Henri gave me the money anyway. He felt my passion and wanted to encourage my dream. He wanted me to try and not give up on something I believed I had to do. And Herb encouraged my dream knowing that I would fail but learn an important lesson along the way.

And I did fail. After many weeks of carefully crafting a generic "Dear Friend" letter addressed to student government presidents around the country, a thousand letters were put in the mail. Each day as I waited for someone to respond my mail box at Dwight Hall remained empty and my dream began to fade. Over the next six months, with my confidence now shattered, sixteen envelopes from a half-dozen schools dribbled in with several dozen checks totaling $14,000.

A mere $484,000 short of my $500,000 goal: *Not the kind of track-record a fundraiser puts on his resume.*

While in my eyes I saw failure, Herb—in his own magical way—saw success! To Herb I had raised $14,000 and gained experience that would be of value to others. Totally ignoring my original goal, Herb began spreading the word that *Henry Freeman knows how to raise money!* Soon students and small non-profits throughout the community were asking for my advice and help. And, I responded, first with small bits of information I gleaned from conversations with other more experienced fundraisers, and then based on my own "trial and error" efforts with various organizations in the community.

As my gifts as a fundraiser began to grow and

develop, I reflected back with wonder and bemusement at my initial enthusiasm and absolute confidence that I would succeed. I also was able to look back and find in that first experience of failure two very important lessons. The first lesson was that fundraising at its best usually starts with a dream that one or more people *cannot* put aside: a dream someone feels *called* or *compelled* to fulfill. In the same way that Henri and Herb responded to my passion, I found myself drawn to the passion and enthusiasm of other people. Their passion for *doing something*—and their ability to communicate *why* they were passionate about what they wanted to do—was in many situations just as compelling as the cause itself.

The second lesson I learned was that the dream cannot be one person's alone. There must be other people who perceive a dream within you and take hold of that dream for themselves. The dream and vision must become something that *we* share together—not something *of mine* that I ask you to support. For that reason, the owner of the dream must see him or herself as a vessel for uncovering how and where the dream also resides in other people. They must be willing to step back and give "ownership" away. That's something many of us find very hard to do.

So in that first experience of failure I learned two

lessons that have served me well throughout my career. Virtually all the other lessons I have acquired in my professional life—about donor pyramids, "how to ask," preparing the case, prospect management, and so on— are simply vehicles that have enabled me to live out and implement the first two lessons I learned through *failure* rather than success.

There is another lesson I learned at Yale that has served me well throughout my professional life. While working with very bright students—many of whom appeared to have the world at their fingertips—I learned to see the vulnerable person that resides in each of us.

Yale was also the place where I met another person named Henry.

—   •   —

"And you won't be lonely anymore."

—Henry

One day while sitting in my office at Dwight Hall, a young woman named Diane Welborn walked in. Outfitted with a warm southern smile and soft accent to match, Diane introduced herself as the wife of a graduate student with some spare time on her hands. After sharing a bit of southern small talk, Diane told me that she and several of her friends loved to bake bread. She

also told me that she met a homeless man two days earlier who asked her for some money so he could buy food.

Out of her love for baking and this one conversation, Diane and her friends decided they would host
a meal for this man and the many other homeless people often seen wondering the streets of inner-city New
Haven. This was not a woman who wanted to "feed
hungry people." Diane was a southern lady who wanted
to *host* meals for people who were hungry. Once you met
Diane you knew you were in the presence of a woman
who knew the difference between welcoming guests and
simply feeding people.

As Diane and I talked, I saw in her a young woman
with a dream. Soon $20 emerged from my desk drawer,
a small room was found at a local church and the Community Soup Kitchen was born.

The launch of the Community Soup Kitchen
started with flyers (paid for with Dwight Hall's $20
bill), which Diane and I pasted up on telephone poles
around New Haven. With Diane and her friends host-
ing a meal for their invited guests on a cold Saturday
morning, the four people who showed up loved the
food, the conversation, and Diane's homemade bread.

The next Saturday, eight people showed up. Then
sixteen. Then two dozen.

By the end of six months, the Community Soup Kitchen moved to a welcoming home in the large activity hall of a local Episcopal Church (still its home forty years later). From that first $20 bill and a young woman's dream the Community Soup Kitchen blossomed! In its new, more spacious quarters, the Soup Kitchen was packed every day Monday through Saturday from noon to two PM with seventy-five to a hundred homeless people and volunteers from the community.

While the budget and numbers of meals served continued to grow over time, one thing about the Community Soup Kitchen did not change. For many people, the Soup Kitchen was not a place to go and receive food. It was a place where people found what we all seek in our lives—a place where we feel welcomed and at home.

Several years later, another group gathered in the outer office of Dwight Hall. This group, mostly students and several people from the local community, wanted to sponsor a Hunger Walk. As plans unfolded the group decided that the Soup Kitchen would be the recipient of half of all the dollars raised.

One person who became very interested in the Hunger Walk was Jane, a junior who dropped by my office one day to tell me that she wanted to help people. What soon emerged from our conversation was the story of a young woman from a wealthy New York family who was trying to find her way in a world where she was privileged in the eyes of society but poor when it came to self-confidence and self-worth.

Very attractive and a bright student, Jane was a person most other people would look at and envy. While I did not know her very well, I imagined her to be a person with lots of friends but few people who really knew the person she saw in the mirror each morning.

Also eager to take part in the Hunger Walk was a young man named Henry who came regularly to the Soup Kitchen. Henry was one of the regulars who fell into the category of being both a guest and a volunteer. One day Henry would be handing out bowls of homemade vegetable soup and the next day he would go through the line receiving soup from others.

The one thing I could count on was that Henry would be at the Soup Kitchen every day at least an hour before it opened. The other thing I could count on was that if we were together, Henry would announce to anyone who would listen that he and I were like brothers because we were both named Henry!

As the day of the Hunger Walk approached, Henry learned that I would be driving a van to pick up people who were having problems completing the 15-mile journey. With little choice in the matter, I accepted Henry's decision to be my partner in what he was convinced would be a glorious adventure. As I pulled up to the Soup Kitchen the morning of the Walk, Henry was excitedly waiting to begin our day together.

Jane, meanwhile, had started on the Walk accompanied by several friends she had asked to join her. To both Jane and Henry, the Hunger Walk was a very big deal. For me it was an event I very much enjoyed, but it was also a Saturday I could have spent with my wife and three-year old twins.

As Henry and I drove down Hamden Avenue halfway on our route, Henry looked over and saw a young woman sitting on the curb with her two friends.

It was Jane. She had sprained her ankle and was waiting for me to drive by and pick her up.

Upon seeing Jane, Henry yelled, "Stop the car!"

As Jane hobbled to her feet, Henry took over. Gently motioning to her friends that he was now in charge, Henry carefully escorted Jane to the back door of the van. After being sure that she was comfortable and not putting pressure on her sprained ankle, Henry got back in the front seat and off we went with Jane and her two friends safely rescued in the back.

The ride at first was filled with laughter when

Henry turned around and informed Jane and her friends that his name was Henry and my name was also Henry but that we were not related. As Henry explained it, we were "like brothers, but not quite."

As Henry's constant talk and the laughter from the back seat continued, the van turned on Dixwell Avenue and we started to drive past the Community Soup Kitchen.

At that point a wonderful, spontaneous, and splendid thing happened: Henry jumped to the window and exclaimed to Jane, her friends and the world, "Jane! Jane! There is the Soup Kitchen! There is the Soup Kitchen! If you are ever lonely or hungry, come down to the Soup Kitchen. We will talk to you and feed you some soup. And you won't be lonely anymore."

The laughter stopped. Tears streamed down from my eyes. In that small transformational moment, Jane and her friends learned what it meant to be welcomed into a community.

They also experienced what it means to be welcomed unconditionally into another person's life.

10

Henri and Herb

A study in contradictions

"But I remember you."

—Henri

Often our life journey weaves together individuals who I think of as a study in contradictions. They are people whose lives bring to the table very similar gifts, yet do so from completely different places of strength.

Herb and Henri were two such people. Henri Nouwen was a Catholic priest and theologian who viewed the world through the lens of a deeply-committed Christian very comfortable talking about Jesus. To Henri, God was always present in his understanding of what it meant to genuinely and deeply be with another person.

Henri's ability to be present for other people also came from a very special place within his own life. In spite of his success and fame, Henri Nouwen was a man who spent his life searching for community but often tried to find it in the wrong places. The academic communities at Harvard and Yale never really understood or embraced what I and many others who knew him would call the "real" Henri. It was not until the last decade of his life that this well-known person found what he spent his life seeking. It was at L'Arche in Ontario, Canada where he lived in community with people who could not read his books that Henri Nouwen found the gift he had given me: a space to be vulnerable. A place where people who loved him were able to come into his life, embrace his vulnerability, accept him as the wounded person he was and, as I learned from Henri, the person we all are.

While Henri Nouwen was a devout Christian and Catholic priest, Herb Cahoon was an agnostic who saw the world through a very different lens. In Herb's eyes, many of the people who call themselves Christians "talk the talk but don't walk the walk." What Herb was interested in was helping people care for other people. To Herb Cahoon, life was no more complicated than that.

One thing Herb and Henri agreed on was that all human beings are broken. While Henri saw our brokenness through the eyes of a priest, Herb saw our human condition through the lens of a man who had spent much of his life prior to Yale as a social worker working with the homeless and walking the halls of Sing Sing prison.

In both men's eyes, there is a place of woundedness in every human being. And it was in that place of vulnerability that both men were at home and present with whomever they shared that sacred space.

— • —

After I left Yale, Herb and I stayed in close touch. While I would occasionally hear that Henri had published another book, more than a decade passed before our next meeting. By then I was vice-president for institutional advancement at Earlham and only months away from my departure for El Salvador. Henri had long ago left Yale and was in the final years of his life living as part of the L'Arche community in Toronto, Canada. While he continued to be a rising star in many religious circles, Henri had finally found a home where he was accepted and loved for no other reason than he was "Henri."

On January 29, 1991, Henri and two companions from the L'Arche Community arrived at the Dayton, Ohio airport. Having been asked by Earlham's president to introduce Henri at the Honorary Doctorate ceremony scheduled for the next day, I greeted Henri and his companions when they got off the plane. Immediately, our relationship picked up where it had ended more than a decade earlier.

As we talked on our drive back to Richmond, I knew that the introduction I had prepared for the next day was all wrong. The man I was prepared to introduce was Henri Nouwen the author and theologian—the person busloads of people from as far away as Chicago were coming to see. We knew from the many calls we had received that Goddard Auditorium would be packed. By now, Henri's reputation had spread around the globe so I was prepared to be as official and scholarly as I was capable of being.

That evening, after a small reception for Henri and his companions, I returned to my office and tore up the five-minute introduction I had spent more than a week preparing. I went to bed not knowing what I was going to say at 10 AM the next morning, when I would be standing in front of more than 1,500 people who would be gathered to hear Henri. What I did know is that I had to return to that place where two decades earlier I had sat in his classroom and found a place where my vulnerability—and Henri's trust in me—had transformed my life.

At three AM I woke up and let my heart speak. As I was to do several months later when sitting with Alfredo on his street corner in El Salvador, I allowed Henri to join me in speaking to each other's heart.

At 10:00 on January 30, 1991, I introduced Henri with the following words:

Earlham College Honorary Degree Convocation
— Henri Nouwen —

It is a deep privilege to stand before you and introduce Henri J. M. Nouwen, a man whose work has influenced countless lives. A man who nearly 20 years ago convinced me to stay in school, gave me my first fundraising donation, and supported me as I pursued one of my most unrealistic dreams. To raise $500,000 for a hospital in Vietnam and I had never raised any money in my life.

A man who for me and numerous others is present through his books at those points in our lives when we struggle with such questions as "who am I?" and "where does God ask me to stand?"

After returning from the airport Sunday evening, Henri, Lavona Godsey, Thelos, Kim, and I broke bread together at Virginia Cottage. Taking advantage of a few empty moments, I asked Henri a question that has long stood dormant in the back of my head.

"Henri J. M. Nouwen. What does the J. M. stand for?"

With a slightly exaggerated grin, Henri informed me that the J. stands for Just and the M. stands for Me.

Henri "Just Me" Nouwen. Author of more than 20 books translated into numerous languages and read by people around the world. Noted priest, psychologist and professor at such schools as Notre Dame, Yale, and Harvard, the middle name "Just Me" hardly fits. Henri is, however, far more than his books and his titles. He is a child of God who has recognized his own brokenness. He is a person who five years ago left the elegant trappings of Harvard University to find community among people whose physical and mental brokenness enabled him to heal his wounds.

Henri J. M. Nouwen is a unique man who brings to us his companions, Kim Barnes and Thelus George, all three members of a very special community where many people cannot read Henri's books and could care less about his Ivy League credentials. It is, indeed, at Daybreak Community in Toronto, Canada where Henri has found a home. It is there that this widely known scholar, teacher, and spiritual guide can be "just me."

Having both been part of the faith community at Yale throughout the 1970s, Henri and I share not only some common history but also a small core of deeply important friends. In preparation for today I called several people who during this period of our lives were very close to Henri and worked with him on several of his books. I would like to share with you some thoughts shared with me by Walter Gaffney, Henri's former assistant at Yale, a good friend, and co-author of one of Henri's books.

> "Henri J. M. Nouwen. You bring spiritual light to thousands in hundreds of places throughout the globe. By making the gift of your life to others you help them to articulate what they have deeply known but have been unable to say. By sharing your search you bring

others to rest. By sharing your pain, you bring others peace. By sharing your loneliness you bring others intimacy. Through your writings, lectures, and retreats, you make the world a hospitable place for many who might otherwise be homeless."

As one of the best known and respected spiritual directors, confessors, and authors in Roman Catholicism today, we at Earlham we are deeply grateful to you for the spiritual direction and guidance you offer this Quaker institution.

Richard Wood, it is an honor to present Henri J. M. Nouwen for the degree of Doctor of Humane Letters.

After the ceremony, I asked Henri if he remembered slipping the envelope with $135 under my door. He said he did not. After a long pause he then looked me in the eyes and said, "But I remember you."

On the drive back to the airport, Henri and I talked about our time together at Yale and my plans to leave in a few months for El Salvador. We then said goodbye to each other for the last time.

A few weeks later I received a short letter from Henri. Busy preparing for my year in El Salvador, I put Henri's letter in a drawer where it waited for me to find time to respond.

Henry Freeman presenting Henri Nouwen with the honorary
degree of Doctor of Humane Letters.
Image captured from video.

That time came many months later.

11

Father Lorenzo

"Thank you, Henri, for being here."

The reality of life in El Salvador did not fully hit me until the day I landed at San Salvador International Airport, entered a van and was driven to a nondescript house in a "middle-class" neighborhood on the outskirts of the city.

I don't remember who greeted me at the airport or all the people I met that first day. What I do remember is my first night in a small 8- by 10-foot room whose simple furnishings included two cot-size beds, a pile of clothes stuffed in one corner, a basketball and a ten-inch high scattering of books that covered every inch of the room's one small table.

Tired from the long flight, I spent most of the evening tossing and turning in the small bed I had claimed as my own. With sleep impossible I woke up every few hours to review my notes from a day of conversation about the reality of life in a country at war. Holding a candle to provide light during one of El Salvador's frequent power outages, I slowly reviewed my penciled list of the things I was expected to always remember: never reveal the location of the house; assume the phone is tapped; avoid using last names in public; always have a taxi or bus drop me off a block or more away from where I am going; avoid any discussion of politics around strangers; and assume that when in a public place (such as a restaurant or bus) someone may be watching who I talk with and trying to listen to what I say.

And—as I was repeatedly told—lower my voice, do not point at another person, and avoid hand gestures that call attention to me or other people.

Before I closed the door and tried to sleep, I learned that the person who claimed the other small bed was an Oblate Priest from Wisconsin named Larry Rosebaugh who spent most of his time in a small village several hours by bus from the capital. While told that we would usually not occupy the small room at the same time (it was a *very* small room), I was assured that I would occasionally see Larry when he ventured into the capital every few weeks for a break from his work as a priest serving his small Salvadoran flock. (For all practical purposes, my first few nights were spent in a "safe house" where I and other church workers within our small group could stay overnight when in the capital.)

My night of rest was short-lived. At 11:00 PM I was awakened by a series of loud explosions followed by a half-hour of sporadic gunfire. Not knowing what to do and without electricity for light, I sat motionless trying to make sense of the noises around me. As I looked into the darkness at the faint outline of the small bed only three feet away, my thoughts kept coming back to my roommate: a man I had never met, knew nothing about, and would not meet for several weeks.

The next morning I learned more about Father Lorenzo Rosebaugh and the world I was now in. Word had arrived a few hours earlier that Larry was being held by a group of soldiers in his small village and that their jokes about burning off his beard with their cigarettes had to be taken seriously. With Larry's life possibly in danger, several people in the house where busy making calls, sending faxes, and trying to activate a network of people back in the States whose telegrams and phone calls were needed to secure his safety. (When working in El Salvador it was critical to have a list of people who could be contacted on short notice if someone disappeared or was in danger. Any delay in making it known that people "cared about a person" could have life or death consequences.)

With conversations about Larry swirling around me I retreated to our small room with little understanding of what was going on. More importantly, I began to ask myself who Larry, the Oblate priest from Wisconsin, *really* was and, of more concern, why I was in El Salvador sharing this small room with a stranger whose life was being threatened.

My first very superficial answer about my roommate was found in the pile of clothes stuffed into one of the room's small corners. As I soon learned, second-hand clothes and his beloved baseball cap were two of Larry's defining trademarks as an unassuming Catholic priest who spent most of his adult life living with the poor in rescue missions and Catholic Worker houses around the United States and in villages needing a priest around the world.

Another side of Larry was also reflected in the basketball that rested in the middle of his small bed. As I soon learned, "Father Lorenzo" as most Salvadorans knew him, had been a promising athlete in his younger days when he was invited to tryout as a catcher for the St. Louis Cardinals. Now a man in his mid-50s, Father Lorenzo's passion for sports focused on basketball—a game he dearly loved and would play on a moment's notice in whatever poverty-stricken area of the world he found himself at home.

Larry was, however, far more than a poorly dressed priest who loved basketball. In the darkness of the little room we shared, I began to explore the many books scattered across the room's only table. It was there among Larry's books that I uncovered a special bond and source of comfort.

Within moments my lighted candle discovered a photograph of hands held together ready to embrace a drink of water or a crumb of bread. It was a simple yet powerful image I had seen twenty years earlier at Yale during a time in my life far removed from the little room I now shared with my unknown roommate.

With candle in hand, I read the title, *With Open Hands.* Then I slowly ran my fingers across the name of the book's author, Henri J. M. Nouwen.

That evening I sat up in my small bed and, by candlelight, wrote Henri a one-page letter. Surrounded by darkness, I told him about the experiences of my first two days in El Salvador, the paralyzing fear I felt, and the comfort I received when I found his words to welcome me into the scary and confusing world I had just entered.

For the next twelve months my letter to Henri occupied a special place in a large canvas bag filled with

the things that were most important to me. While I
no longer remember all the details of the letter I do
remember my opening words: "Thank you, Henri, for
being here."

Over the course of my year in El Salvador, Larry
and I became close friends. While at times our conversation was about Henri, my life as a fundraiser or Larry's
life as a priest more often our time together centered
around a game of basketball on a makeshift dirt court
or the Salvadoran fried chicken we always ordered at a
little open air restaurant down the street.

More importantly, Larry was a person I could talk
to about my fears and my dreams. He, like Henri, was
a gifted listener.

For several years after I left El Salvador and returned
to the States, Larry and I remained in touch through a
mutual friend. Then, three years ago, I learned that Larry
was murdered in 2009 by masked gunmen while working
and living with the poor in Guatemala.

Father Lorenzo was 74 years old when he died.

—   •   —

With regret, I never sent Henri the letter I wrote
on that lonely night in El Salvador. As is true of many
things in life, the letter disappeared after I returned to

the States—either thrown out with a misplaced pile of papers or, perhaps, still waiting for me between the pages of a long-forgotten book.

In 1996 Henri died from a heart attack while in Holland visiting his father. Unlike Alfredo, who lies somewhere in an unmarked grave, Henri's body was returned to Canada where he is buried in a cemetery near his beloved L'Arch Daybreak community. He was 64 years old when he died.

Several years ago I had the privilege of visiting Daybreak and meeting many of Henri's friends. There, surrounded by members of Henri's community, I heard stories about a man who was universally remembered for two things: his terrible driving (as one person repeatedly stated, "Henri was always talking. He *never* watched the road!") and the fact that this famous theologian was not very gifted at anything to do with domestic chores! More importantly, there was lots of laughter and joyful conversation about a man fondly remembered for the love in his heart. A man who made the decision to leave the scholarly life of Yale and Harvard to spend the last years of his life living with people who could not read his books and couldn't care less about his fame.

There, in a cemetery near Daybreak, Henri is surrounded by people who loved him for the person he was and the person I was privileged to know.

Henri "Just Me" Nouwen.

12
A final kiss on
an old man's head

Then, on David and Sara's thirtieth
birthday, the phone was silent.
"Old Man Cahoon" forgot to call.

On Sunday, August 17, 2008, I had dinner with Herb and Jean Cahoon at their home in Woodbridge, Connecticut. At the end of an evening of good conversation and shared memories, I told Herb what a positive impact he had exerted on my life. I then kissed him on top of his head and said, for the first time, "I love you."

The next morning, Herb died. He had lived a good life. He was ninety-one years old.

I spent that afternoon with Jean, back at their home. Between periods of comfortable silence, Jean and I told old stories and shared long-held memories of Herb.

Our time together the day Herb died was very special for both of us. For Jean it was a time to mourn the loss of her husband of 63 years and share cherished memories of their relationship. For me, it was a time to grieve the loss of my mentor and friend—a time to dig deep into my heart and explore memories of a man who had a lasting impact on the course of my life.

At Jean's request, I returned to Yale one month later to officiate at Herb's memorial service. In front of the many friends and former students gathered in Dwight Chapel, I told those present about the kiss I'd placed on top of Herb's bald head. I also told them how privileged I was to be able to tell Herb I loved him the night before he died and share with Jean the precious and tender moments in the hours after his death.

Following the memorial service for my mentor and friend, I knew there was something more I needed to share. For the next nine months, I was convinced that that "something" was the knowledge and skills I possess as a fundraiser. Gradually, however, I began to realize what I have to share is far more universal and important. Indeed, it has less to do with fundraising and more to do with how you and I relate to other people, our work and our careers.

At its core, what I have tried to share in this book is not what we learn with our heads but a gift we receive with our hearts. It is the gift of being invited into another person's life; an invitation to be "present" in a vulnerable space where our walls come down and our masks are taken off.

A space where human beings connect and lives are transformed.

13

Connecting with what really matters in our lives and careers

"The person is more important than the problem, and the relationship is more important than the solution."

—William Oglesby

Early one morning many years ago, I went into my office and noticed that a new message had been left on my phone answering machine. The time of the message was 12:15 AM.

The person who left the message was a nurse at a retirement community in Hendersonville, North Carolina. The female voice simply stated,

"Esther died this morning at 12:09 AM. She wanted you to know."

My relationship with Esther and her husband, Robert, was unique in two ways. First, they lived in a retirement community only twenty miles from my aging parents so I got to visit with them four to six times each year, which was more often than I visited with most other donors. They also were people who found it odd that I was a fundraiser (and a seemingly intelligent person) who nonetheless believed in God. (Like Herb, Robert took great joy in kidding me about going to divinity school. To Robert, as long as I wasn't a "pastor" I was probably okay.)

The real substance and uniqueness of our relationship, however, unfolded where I find it usually does with the people I meet. As with most donors, it occurred in a private place where we were able to explore the sacred space that connected us as human beings.

It was in that shared space that Esther and Robert felt comfortable unfolding about their lives and their lifelong disappointment over not being able to have children. (Helping children was their passion and providing scholarships for students was a source of great satisfaction in their lives.)

Our conversations, however, went far beyond their desire to provide scholarships that would help other people's children attend college. It was in the sacred space we built together that Robert shared with me his struggles as a young boy who lost his sight in an accident

when he was five years old. It was in that space that
Robert and Esther found in me a person eager to hear
their inner stories, including those that had absolutely
nothing to do with Earlham, my work as a fundraiser,
or anything remotely associated with why I was sitting
in their living room.

It was through their stories that there emerged a deep
and heartfelt connection to me and my journey as a person.
It was in this safe place that they found in me a person who
genuinely and authentically cared about them as people
who—like Alfredo—had stories to share but few people
who would take the time to listen.

It was in that sacred space that a bond developed
that led to the message on my answering machine six
minutes following Esther's death. And, it was in that
sacred space several years earlier that Robert saw in me
the person he wanted to have his pocket watch after he
died.

It was a pocket watch without a glass cover, so that
the soft touch of a blind man's fingers could keep track
of the time and rhythms of his life.

Was my relationship with Esther and Robert
unique? Absolutely. But was the depth of my relationship with Esther and Robert a rare experience?

Absolutely not.

The great joy for me as a fundraiser is that my career has enabled me to enter such relationships with many, many people.

One of the things I have learned over the course of my 35-year career is that my desire to leave a visit with a financial commitment in hand often can be the very thing that gets in the way of the stories and conversations that lead to truly sacrificial and transformational gifts. When, however, I approach my visits with a donor as a joyful opportunity to explore what is most important to them—which often contains some "thread" or story that is interwoven with the mission of the organization I represent—the gifts flow. Most are very small in size but very meaningful to a person of modest means. Others, however, are six- and seven-figure gifts received from a person I have known a relatively short period of time. (Contrary to what many people believe, It is not the amount of time with a donor or the number of visits that matters. Deeply meaningful stories that blossom into very large financial investments are often "just below the surface" in a person's heart, waiting to be discovered and shared.)

The problem for most of us is that, too often, we enter the lives of another person with an agenda that narrowly defines the relationship around what we want to talk about rather than what is in the heart of the person we are meeting with. As a result, we have very nice and cordial meetings that rarely get to the heart of a person's deepest feelings and passions.

The reality is that most people do not want to connect with me or any other fundraiser at more than a rather superficial level. That is to be expected and should be of no surprise to anyone. There are, however, many people who yearn to find someone who is open to entering "that space" where they can remove their walls and genuinely and authentically be present with another human being.

Unfortunately, many people in my profession are hesitant to share that sacred space with people when the door is opened and they are invited in. For some, the barriers to entering that door are deeply personal and grounded in experiences of woundedness and hurt from other relationships. Others believe that "getting personal" is not something a professional person should do and that doing so will be harmful to their career.

The barriers to building truly deep relationships that most people face in my profession are very similar to the barriers faced by clergy, teachers, nurses, social workers and others engaged in the "helping professions." What is most troubling is that what draws many of us to these professions—the belief that we will connect with other people at a deeply meaningful level—is often not what we find and experience. For many of us, the problem may be that our work environment has been "taken over" by expectations and demands that have little to do with the core work of our profession. In some cases, we may even ask ourselves, "Does my job *allow me* to build genuine and sincere relationships with people?"

For fundraisers and members of most professions, the "hat we wear" clearly states that our presence in the room with another human being is primarily grounded in what we do to pay the bills. Indeed, few people will trust you (nor should they) if at any point you try to disown the professional role that brings you to their door and into their lives.

There are, however, many opportunities to move relationships to a deeper level while still working within the boundaries framed by the professional roles we play. Those moments are most often found in the small invitations people extend to see them as a person who needs your presence as well as your expertise, the skills you possess, and the agenda you bring with you when you arrive at their door.

Few of us can toss aside the "head stuff" that weighs heavily on our daily lives—the paperwork, dollar goals, and/or the numbers of people we serve or visit on any given day. What we *can* control is our willingness and desire to genuinely and authentically be present with another person for whatever time and in whatever space we occupy with them.

I am sure there are people who read these stories and see me as a person living a life far removed from their own. But is my life—and the people I have met—really that different from your life and the people you interact with each day?

If you take the time to slow down and listen, you will open yourself up to a world where there are many Alfredos with outstretched arms waiting to welcome you into their lives. Some are visibly broken people like Mary, who wanders the streets and struggles to make sense of a terrifying world around her. Others are very wealthy people with millions of dollars that hide the poverty and loneliness they feel inside—people who fear that their money is the only thing that people care about. Still others are like Margaret, sitting in a retirement home late in life waiting for someone to be present with them as they enter the last stages of their life journey.

As you look around, you will also see young people like Jane who found in Henry someone who would joyfully welcome her to a place where she would be served a cup of soup and be lonely no more. And there are many children like Ricardo who need someone to sit beside them as they struggle with painful memories of a lost or damaged family.

And then there are people like me, who found in three friends the strength to share these stories with you.

And there are people like you, who—like all of us—has a story to share with someone who will listen.

Epilogue

Finding our way to
what matters in life

In the safety of our home, my father asked the all-important question,

> "Who is our neighbor and what does it mean
>   to love and respect that person?"

As I put words to paper for this book I often found myself drifting back into memories from my childhood. Several experiences from more than a half century ago provide a window into why I have shared these stories with you.

Growing up in the Deep South in the 1950s where segregated schools and whites only drinking fountains were a daily part of life, very few people talked about race. For the vast majority of good and caring people (and there were *many* good and caring people) in our

100

community segregation was simply the way our world was and, for that reason, it was generally accepted as how the world was meant to be.

One early memory is of my grandfather—a man I dearly loved—being puzzled by the ever growing conversation about civil rights that seeped into our living room through the screen of our black and white TV. Sitting in his favorite chair as he watched the evening news with the rest of our family in the 1950s, my grandfather would occasionally express the views of most people in our community. While I don't remember his exact words, he was one of the many people who simply didn't see a problem since, in his eyes, "We all seem to get along just fine."

My grandfather did not speak with the voice of a person filled with hate. His were the soft and gentle words of an elderly man who lived in a community blind to the evil around us. A community where a racist joke was seen as funny rather than hurtful and people from the outside who questioned our way of life simply didn't know what life in the South was *really* like.

While race was the most visible wall that divided our community, our world was also tightly controlled by other less obvious barriers. When I was growing up a woman was defined more by the profession of her husband, the cleanliness of her house and the taste of the fried chicken she brought to a church picnic than her talents and inherent worth as a person. My mother, for example, was an accomplished poet and writer who for most of my childhood had a syndicated column that appeared three times each week in over 200 newspapers around the country. Sadly, my mother struggled for most of her adult life with the fear that her success as a writer and poet might overshadow her assigned role as a wife and a mother. (One important clause in my mother's contract with King Features Syndicate was that her column *could not* be carried in any paper widely available in our local community.)

In keeping with what she accepted as her primary role in life, my mother's column was titled "At Our House," where for ten years she shared with the world small moments in our Ozzie-and-Harriet–like family about my father going off to work each day, her view of our backyard from the kitchen window, and small insights into the lives of little boys as they fished for bluegill in a nearby pond.

The world my mother shared in her column and poems was in many ways a real life snapshot of the life I experienced in our family. What was not shared in those early years was the other reality of life in our community:

a world in which my mother always played down her gifts as a poet and frequently felt compelled to announce (even on stage when invited to read her poetry) that first and foremost she was a wife and a mother who saw her writing as a secondary calling. Perhaps for that reason, her poetry during my childhood years focused on what she labeled as "happy things"—a baby's small fingers, the joy of being a housewife, or the story of a small boy playing basketball with friends in our backyard.

In spite of my father's unwavering support and encouragement of her professional life as a poet and writer, it was not until I was an adult that my mother broke free from her southern upbringing to share powerful insights into the darker side of small town life in the South.

Below is one example of the raw and compelling poetry for years buried deep in my mother's heart. Appearing in an appropriately titled book, *No Costumes or Masks,* my mother (by then a woman in her late 50s) ran free with deeply held memories of a shameful time in her childhood.

Small White Cannibal

With my weekly nickel
begged from the long leather
change purse, flat and lean

as my father the Depression
had honed bone sharp.
I could buy a handful of Nigger Babies,
stand in the candy store
before the fly-specked glass case
and guillotine with my teeth
the heads from their chocolate bodies.
Sometimes I chomped from the other end,
leaving only the small round face
to mash to a chewy ball
and toss into the air.
If it missed my mouth
and rolled instead beneath the counter,
I did not bother to cry.
Mr. Ned would give me another.
They don't sell them now,
but back then Nigger Babies
came cheap.

—*Grace Beacham Freeman*

"Small White Cannibal" was first published in 1975. Two decades later, my mother and I spent a quiet afternoon reflecting back on her life and the power of her poetry. Now 80 years old and in failing health, my mother shared with me her memory of another child in Mr. Ned's store that day long ago. As if only yesterday, she talked about the little African American boy half her age who stood silently in a corner several feet away as my mother innocently enjoyed her candy.

— • —

The most obvious walls in our community defined a person's role by race and gender. Many other walls, however, were also constructed to keep people apart and shape our view of the world around us. Social status was certainly one. The other most prominent wall was defined by what church you attended. In our community, a Sunday School lesson might very well have included a statement about Catholics worshipping idols or why baptism by immersion is what separates the true Christian from those whose faith is based on a false interpretation of the Bible.

The walls that filled our community did exactly what walls do. They kept people apart and led to our not seeing the evil as it existed right in front of our noses.

The only time our church opened its doors on a Sunday morning to the African American community was on Race Relations Day when a single black pastor and his wife were invited to join us for worship. Even then I remember several people walking out, including one of my best friends. More importantly, that same pastor knew he and his wife would be politely turned away if they tried to worship with us any other day of the year. (Until my early teen years, this was true of every white church in our community.)

Fortunately, in my own family, the sermon I heard

in church on Sunday morning was often followed by
conversations around our dining room table where my
father, a college professor, would seek from the Good
Samaritan story and other biblical passages a deeper level
of meaning. In the safety of our home he would ask an
all-important question, "Who is our neighbor—right
here in our community—and what does it mean to love
and respect that person?"

My father's understanding of the Good Samaritan
story presented an alternative—and, in the eyes of some
people, dangerous—view of the world around us. The
conversations we had around our dining room table also
opened my eyes to religion and faith as a journey into
deep and challenging questions rather than simple and
easy answers.

Recalling these conversations with my father brings
back several painful memories. One is of two women in
front of our church when as a small boy I overheard them
talking about my father, a man they viewed with suspicion
because he was believed to hold "dangerous" views about
race and how the teachings of Jesus related to the changing
world around us. Views that may have been particularly
threatening because my father was not a stranger they could
easily ignore. He was a deacon in their church who collected
the church offering, taught Sunday School, and sang each

week in the church choir.

Years later, I told my father about this experience. It was then, as an adult, that I learned that my father had served on the board of a local museum and had proposed that black parents and their children be allowed to use this tax-funded facility. While his resolution was approved—with permission granted for black families to visit the museum on Saturdays only—my father's actions were considered by some to be a dangerous and radical challenge to our community values and way of life.

Another memory still with me more than a half century later occurred in the pet department of McCrory's variety store on Main Street, a frequent Saturday morning destination for a ten-year-old boy eager to find one more turtle or pair of guppies for his animal collection.

For as long as I can remember, McCrory's pet department was a magical world of hamsters, snakes, and tropical fish where I lived out my dream of being a biologist like my father. It was, however, also the place where the values I was taught at home first clashed with the harsh reality of the world outside our front door.

Each time I visited McCrory's and walked down the long aisle to the pet department, I was greeted by a drinking fountain with a large sign announcing it was for "Colored Only." Having innocently learned from my father that the world we lived in was not as it should be, I decided that one day I would take the small defiant step of drinking from that fountain. That day came one Saturday morning when, at age ten, I stepped up on the stool reserved for black children, pressed the button and took a sip of water. Thinking I was alone, I was not surprised by the few quiet moments that followed. Then I heard a loud voice behind me.

At first I thought the big man was angry. He was not. He was laughing.

Laughing at a small white boy he assumed did not see the sign.

I never told my father—or anyone—what happened that day, or how I felt when a stranger laughed at me for doing what I believed was right.

— • —

Recently, after a fifty year absence, my two brothers and sister returned to the church of our childhood to attend the funeral for one of our mother's life-long friends. Overwhelmed with emotion when he saw the church filled with all shades of skin color, my younger brother David wept as he uncovered his own memories of a childhood when, in eleventh grade, Martin Luther King's death was greeted with laughter and celebration by many of his classmates.

To be clear, my brother and I have many positive memories of a loving childhood filled with lots of friends and a caring family. While the worst of the segregated south was abundantly present during our school years, the small southern town we remember was mostly filled with pickup football, swimming at the YMCA, and neighbors who knew that seven-year-old David and ten-year-old Henry—like every other child in our neighborhood—had to be home each evening at 6:00 PM for a sit-down meal with their family.

It was in our childhood—both for good and for bad—that the seeds were planted for who my brother and I are today. Seeds grounded in a tension between the faith we gleaned from our father—a faith grounded in asking the hard questions—and the religious beliefs and attitudes that held sway in the world just beyond our front door.

Brother David's painful memories of years long past laid the foundation for both his rejection of religion altogether and his maturation into one of the most ethical and caring people I have ever known. For me, my path took a different turn. At the age of 19, my childhood experiences led me to Friends (also known as Quakers), a faith community that, like my father, seeks to find that of God in every human being including those whose beliefs and way of life we don't understand and may even fear.

The wounds my brother and I experienced more than a half century ago are mere pinpricks when compared to the debilitating and painful scars borne by many children. They are, however, part of who we are today and who we will become in the future.

Having such wounds is one of the things that makes all of us human and is part of the baggage every person carries through life. As we all know, wounds can leave lasting scars that cause us to build higher and higher walls carefully constructed to keep the world out. Wounds, however, can also be a gift.

A gift that transforms our life and empowers us to see the world through a very different lens.

Made in the USA
Middletown, DE
11 May 2017